Put on Your Thinking Cap

And Other Expressions about SCHOOL

MATT DOEDEN

Illustrated by

AARON BLECHA

Lerner Publications Company

MINNEAPOLIS

Lerner Publications Company
A division of Lerner Publishing Group, Inc.
241 First Avenue North
Minneapolis, MN 55401 U.S.A.

Website address: www.lernerbooks.com

Library of Congress Cataloging-in-Publication Data

Doeden, Matt.
    Put on your thinking cap: And other expressions
  about school / by Matt Doeden.
      p.   cm. — (It's just an expression)
    Includes index.
    ISBN 978-0-7613-7891-4 (lib. bdg. : alk. paper)
    1. English language—Idioms—Juvenile literature.
  2. Figures of speech—Juvenile literature. 3. Schools.
  I. Title.
  PE1460.D64 2013
  428.1—dc23   2011040792

Manufactured in the United States of America
1 – PC – 7/15/12

TABLE of CONTENTS

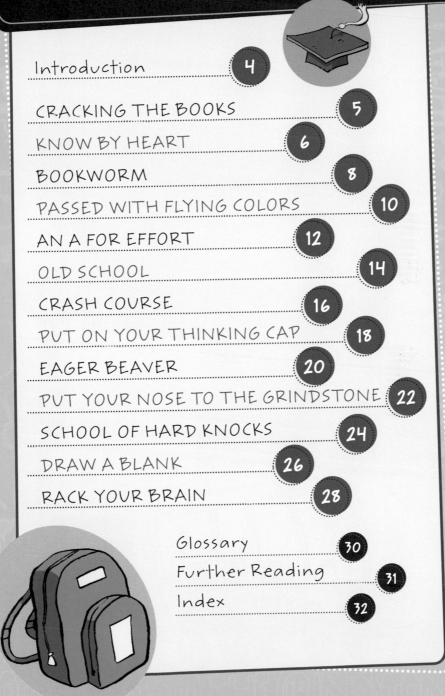

INTRODUCTION

"Woot! Woot!" said Hailey when the teacher handed back her social studies test. "I got an A! How awesome is that?"

"Congratulations!" answered Hailey's friend Abby. "But I'm *so* not surprised. You've been **cracking the books** all week. You know all the state capitals **by heart.** I knew you'd **pass with flying colors!**"

What on earth is Abby talking about? Cracking the books? Knowing capitals by heart? Flying colors? It sounds as if she's speaking a different language. But she's not. Abby's just using idioms. <u>Idioms are phrases that mean something different from what you might think they mean.</u> Sometimes they can seem super confusing. But once you learn what idioms mean—and where the phrases come from—they're not so weird-sounding after all. So read on to take **a crash course** in idioms. Soon they'll seem as easy as ABC!

CRACKING the BOOKS

"Hey, Tyler," Mason greeted his next-door neighbor. "Wanna come over and play Xbox with me?"

"Yeah, dude, but I can't," Tyler replied. "My mom said I have to crack the books tonight."

"Too bad, bud," Mason answered.

What does Tyler mean he has to crack the books? Books are for reading, not cracking, right?

Relax—Tyler's mom isn't suggesting that he break his books in half. **When you crack a book, it just means that you open it and read it.** That's all Tyler's mom wants him to do. She says he should spend more time on homework and less on gaming (which Tyler isn't too thrilled about).

So why do we use the phrase *crack the books* to describe opening a book? It's because sometimes, when a new hardcover book is opened for the first time, its spine makes a cracking sound. So if you crack a book, it means that you've started to read it. Now that makes a lot more sense than splitting a book in two, doesn't it?

This kid's stuck cracking the books when he'd rather be playing Xbox.

KNOW by HEART

Bao practiced and practiced for her oboe solo. But on the day she was supposed to play in front of the whole school, she felt nervous.

"I'm afraid I'm going to make a mistake in the assembly!" she told her friend Hannah. "Don't worry," Hannah reassured her. "You totally know your solo by heart. You're going to do awesome."

Now, no one doubts that your heart's a pretty useful organ. It pumps blood to every cell in your body! But as strong as your heart is, it's not particularly good at learning things. It just sits there in your chest thump-thump-thumping away. So what does Hannah mean?

When you know something by heart, it means you've got it memorized. You don't even have to think about it. Suppose you know a favorite poem or your multiplication tables by heart. That means you don't need any help in reciting the material. You can easily repeat the information. But why does the phrase *know by heart* mean that you really know something? We've got to look back thousands of years to ancient Greece for the answer.

The ancient Greeks believed that the heart was the center of all thought and feeling. So to learn something by heart was to know it completely. In modern times, we know we learn with our brains, not our hearts. But we still like the idea of learning something by heart, so the idiom lives on.

If you recite something from memory, you know it by heart.

BOOKWORM

Ryan was reading at the dinner table again. His family didn't mind too much—except when they needed him to pass the peas. "You're such a bookworm, Ry," his dad said with a smile. "You'd read all day long if you could!"

What does Ryan's dad mean by calling him a bookworm? Worms are slimy, and some people think they're kind of gross. All Ryan wanted was to find out how his novel ended. That hardly seems like a good reason to call him names.

Of course, Ryan's dad doesn't really mean his son's a worm. **Bookworm is just a nickname for someone who spends a lot of time reading.** It isn't an insult at all!

Kids who love to read are often called bookworms.

But where does the term *bookworm* come from? It's actually pretty simple. It comes from insects that eat books. Bugs such as book lice and silverfish sometimes get into books. They eat the paste that holds the book's binding together. Obviously, they spend a lot of time in books. It isn't hard to figure out how the term came to mean someone who spends a lot of time reading.

Creepy-crawly bugs such as this one like to eat the paste that holds books together.

What would you do if you saw this six-legged critter in your book? (Don't worry—this book is bug free. We hope.)

PASSED with FLYING COLORS

Kylie had to take a test to move up to the next level in gymnastics. She worked really hard to master all her skills, and her coach said that she passed with flying colors.

What kind of test did Kylie take, anyway? Was it some sort of bizarre crayon-throwing test? As fun as that might sound, Kylie didn't have to throw crayons to prove to her coach that she was ready to advance. But how else would she get colors to fly?

You don't need to actually make anything fly to pass with flying colors. **This idiom just means you've accomplished something easily and with great success.** Scoring 100 percent on your pop quiz in math would mean you

This young gymnast passed her gymnastics test with flying colors.

passed with flying colors. So would getting a perfect grade on your history report.

OK—so now you know what it means to pass with flying colors. But where does this phrase come from? It comes from an era before cars, trucks, and planes existed. Back then, ships were a main means of transportation. They crossed oceans and traveled up and down rivers. <u>Sailors raised bright, colorful flags to identify their ships. These flags were often called colors.</u> When a ship came into port or passed another ship, the flags would blow in the wind. For many sailors, serving aboard a fast ship was a source of pride. They loved to watch their colors fly. Similarly, Kylie's coach was pleased to see her "flying" through her gymnastics routine.

Centuries ago, ships sported brightly colored flags to help identify the vessels.

An A for EFFORT

Abdullah's mom tried to buy him some cool jeans. But the jeans just weren't what Abdullah had in mind. "I know she tried, but I think I want to return them," Abdullah told his older sister. "I do give Mom an A for effort, though."

Abdullah may be giving his mom a grade, but it doesn't count like the ones he gets in school. In fact, all he's saying is that she tried, but didn't quite succeed, when it came to buying him some cool jeans. **Saying that you give someone an A for effort means that you appreciate the work that he or she put into a task.** It's kind of a good news/bad news deal, though. That's because it also means you think the end result wasn't very good.

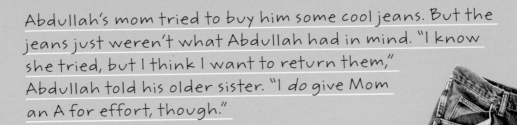

Imagine that you try to fix your friend's bike. You spend hours tinkering with it and tuning it, trying to get it just right. But in the end, the bike is in even worse shape than when you started. Your friend might tell you he gives you an A for effort. <u>You worked hard and did your best. But in the end, you didn't accomplish what you set out to accomplish.</u> Still, at least you tried!

This guy's trying hard to fix his friend's bike—but shhh! The truth is that he has no clue what he's doing!

OLD SCHOOL

"Hey, Maura!" Cecelia shouted when she saw her best friend at the bus stop. "My mom let me download the most awesome song last night. I'll play it for you later. It's by Cyndi Lauper."

Maura laughed and rolled her eyes affectionately at her friend.

"Isn't Cyndi Lauper from the '80s?" she asked. "Cece, you're so old school."

What does Maura mean by calling her friend old school? Is she saying that Cecelia's old? And what does school have to do with anything?

Old school is a way of describing someone who likes things from the past. Old-school people often don't care about the latest fashions or trends. They stick with what they like and ignore the crowd.

Cyndi Lauper is a singer who was super popular in the '80s. You might call her current fans old school.

An old-school person also might like to do things in a traditional way. For example, say your teacher insists that you do your homework with pencil and paper instead of on a computer. You might say that he's old school.

How did *old school* come to mean old fashioned? It comes from the world of academics. In academics, there are all kinds of different theories and ideas. People who work in academics tend to be passionate about the theories and ideas they believe in. Those with similar beliefs are said to belong to the same schools, or groups, of thought. And those who support older ideas instead of newer ones are said to be old school.

This teacher's really old school. He makes his students write reports by hand.

CRASH COURSE

"My laptop broke last night, but I figured out how to fix it," Kaden told his friend Jeff. "I got a crash course in computer repair!"

Did Kaden really take a course to figure out how to fix his computer? And what's a crash course, anyway? Does it have to do with smashing things? Kaden *did* kind of feel like smashing his computer when it started acting up as he was finishing his book report.

If you took a crash course on computer repair, it means you learned how to fix a computer in a hurry.

No, Kaden didn't take a course on laptop repair. He didn't crash—or smash—anything either. **He just means that he had to learn how to fix his laptop very quickly when it broke down unexpectedly.**

Where does the saying *crash course* come from? No one's quite sure. <u>But most people seem to think it comes from someone having to learn to land a crashing airplane.</u> Just imagine it. You're flying an airplane, and it's going down. You've got to figure out how to land it, or you might wind up dead. Talk about pressure! This scenario may very well explain why we use the phrase *crash course* when we need to learn something in a hurry.

The phrase *crash course* may come from pilots. If a plane has mechanical problems while it's in the air, a pilot has to figure out quickly how to land it.

PUT on YOUR THINKING CAP

Jayne's teacher had just arranged the class into groups. Each group was supposed to come up with an idea for a science project. Then the people in each group were supposed to work together to finish their projects and present them to the class. "We'll have to put on our thinking caps to come up with a good idea for our project," Jayne said to the members of her group.

Caps, helmets, bonnets, and beanies—there are many different kinds of hats. But why does Jayne want her group members to wear one? And how are hats supposed to help them think?

Jayne doesn't actually want anyone to wear a hat. **When you put on your thinking cap, you're just getting ready to think really hard about a problem.** Maybe you've got to think of a birthday present for your best friend. Or maybe you need to figure out how to trick your brother into switching rooms with you. If you need your thinking cap, get ready to do some hard-core thinking!

Why do we use the phrase *put on your thinking cap* when we just mean that you'll have to think hard? It may be because of the special hats that English judges wore in the seventeenth century. The hats were called considering caps. Judges wore them while deciding on a criminal's sentence. According to some accounts, judges wouldn't speak a word as long as they were wearing the caps. They'd wait to speak until they'd thought through the problem.

This fifth-grade graduate is headed straight to middle school!

EAGER BEAVER

José walked up to his teacher's desk as his classmates were busily reading a short story. "Mr. Smith," he said in a quiet voice. "I've already finished reading the story. Do you have any extra credit I could do?"

"Wow, José," replied Mr. Smith. "You're certainly an eager beaver! You'll find questions about the story in your reading textbook. You may answer those for extra credit."

José's teacher seemed impressed that José asked for extra work. But why did he call him a beaver? Does José have giant teeth like a beaver? Does he spend a lot of time chewing trees?

Nah, José's actually a pretty normal kid—although his friends *do* joke that he must have superpowers because he reads so quickly! So what gives?

Does this beaver look eager to you?

An eager beaver is just someone who works really hard. It's a person who has a lot of enthusiasm and puts effort into getting ahead. That certainly describes José.

This idiom became popular during World War II (1939– 1945). Some soldiers in that war always seemed to be trying to impress their commanding officers. They were always busy. They reminded some of their fellow soldiers of beavers. These furry rodents are often hard at work building beaver dams. Since *eager beaver* sort of rhymes and is fun to say, the idiom quickly spread.

This kid's an eager beaver. He always has the answers when his teacher asks a question!

PUT YOUR NOSE to the GRINDSTONE

"I have a ton of math homework tonight," Chloe told her mom at dinner. "I don't know how I'm going to get it all done."

"Don't worry," her mom replied. "I know you'll finish your assignment. You'll just need to put your nose to the grindstone."

What exactly is a grindstone, and why does Chloe's mom want her to put her nose to one? That sounds as if it might be painful. Chloe would rather take an incomplete if finishing her assignment means she has to grind her nose off!

Chloe doesn't have to worry—and neither do you if someone tells you to put your nose to the grindstone. **This idiom just means that you**

If you have a ton of homework, you might have to put your nose to the grindstone.

need to really concentrate. When you put your nose to the grindstone, you block out all distractions. You focus on your work until the job is done. (And, sure, this isn't always easy—but it's definitely a whole lot easier than grinding off your nose!)

So now you know what the idiom means. But where does it come from? Most people think it refers to a method that people once used to sharpen knives. They'd hold the knife blades against a large, spinning stone. Often they kept their faces very close to the stone to get the best results. They had to focus hard on holding the knife at the right angle to make sure the blade got sharp. Similarly, Chloe has to focus on her math to make sure the problems get done correctly and on time.

SCHOOL of HARD KNOCKS

Mike's dad was always telling him how important it was to save money. He often told Mike about how he'd had a job in high school but wasted all the money he'd earned on things he didn't need. "I learned about saving money from the school of hard knocks," he said to his son.

Where *is* the school of hard knocks, anyway? Is it hard to get into? Do they have a good track-and-field team?

You've probably guessed the answer already. The school of hard knocks isn't really a school at all. **It's just an expression that means a person has learned through life experiences—often difficult ones.** People often use the term to compare life lessons to formal education. The idea is that they've learned from tough situations in ways they probably couldn't learn at school.

Writer George Ade created the term hard knocks in 1912. It appeared in his story "The Heir and the Heiress." The term described a setback in life. Modern writers might use the term *raw deal* in a similar way.

Whether you call it a hard knock or a raw deal, a tough situation is a good thing to avoid. That's why Mike's dad likes to tell him (over and over again!) not to make the same mistake he made.

George Ade (above) first used the term *hard knocks* in his story "The Heir and the Heiress."

In this scene from the musical *Annie*, the characters sing a song called "It's the Hard-Knock Life."

DRAW a BLANK

Samantha's teacher, Mrs. Anderson, asked her when the Pilgrims came to America. Samantha knew the answer was 1620—but when she saw her classmates' eyes on her, she got nervous. "I-I'm sorry," stuttered Samantha. "I can't remember the answer."

"That's OK, Sam," said Mrs. Anderson, who was everyone's favorite teacher. "Everybody draws a blank sometimes. Fatima, can you help us out?"

What did Mrs. Anderson mean when she said that everybody draws a blank? How exactly does one draw a blank? You can draw lots of things—houses, rainbows, and animals, to name a few. But what would a blank look like? And why would anyone want to draw one?

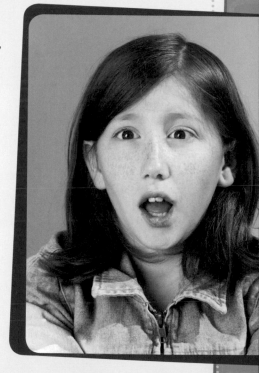

Put your pencils away. There's no drawing needed to understand this idiom. **To draw a blank is to fail to remember something.** When you draw a blank, you've got the knowledge somewhere in your brain. You just can't manage to recall it. It can be pretty frustrating!

We have to look back to England of the late 1500s to see where this idiom comes from. Queen Elizabeth I started a national lottery to raise money. People wrote their names on tickets and then dropped them into a pot. An equal number of prize tickets went into another pot. Some of the prize tickets had names of prizes written on them. Others were blanks. One ticket from each pot was drawn. <u>If your name was drawn along with a ticket that had a prize name written on it, you were a winner. If you drew a blank, you lost.</u> Too bad for you!

The phrase *draw a blank* got started in the time of Queen Elizabeth I. If you draw a blank, don't feel too bad. Probably even old Elizabeth drew a blank sometimes.

RACK YOUR BRAIN

The pop quiz really caught Jake by surprise. "I had to rack my brain to remember the answers," he told his friend Toby over lunch.

Hold on a second. Jake had to do *what* to his brain? A rack is all well and good if we're talking about a clothing store at the mall. But as nice and orderly as racks may be, they hardly seem like a place for a perfectly good brain.

Of course, Jake didn't really put his brain on a rack. **The expression *rack your brain* just means that you're trying your hardest to remember something or to figure something out.** You may have to squint your eyes and grunt and groan a little, but your brain itself stays safely in your head.

Although your brain isn't in any danger if you rack it, the idiom *rack your brain* does have a dark history. Centuries ago, a rack was a tool used to stretch something out—leather, for example. Later, the rack became a terrible torture device. An unlucky person was placed on a rack to have his or her arms and legs painfully stretched to get information. The idea was that the pain would force the person to tell all. <u>As time went on, the idiom rack your brain came to mean stretching one's brain to remember something.</u> Sometimes, people spell it *wrack* instead of rack. *Wrack* is another word for wreck. Either way, it's a pretty unpleasant image. Luckily, it's just an expression!

Racks like this one were used for stretching leather. Can you imagine putting your brain on one? Yeeow!

Glossary

academics: the field of studying and learning

ancient: very old, or belonging to a time long ago

idiom: a commonly used expression or phrase that means something different from what it appears to mean

school of thought: a group of people who support the same theories or ideas

theory: an idea or statement that explains how or why something happens

Further Reading

Amoroso, Cynthia. *I'm All Thumbs! (And Other Odd Things We Say)*. Mankato, MN: Child's World, 2011. Learn more about some of the English language's strangest idioms and why we say the things we say.

Atkinson, Mary. *What Do You Mean? Communication Isn't Easy*. New York: Children's Press, 2007. Learn about all sorts of things that can make communication confusing, from idioms and changing word meanings to jargon and dialects.

Doeden, Matt. *Stick Out Like a Sore Thumb: And Other Expressions about Body Parts*. Minneapolis: Lerner Publications Company, 2013. If you liked reading about school idioms, you'll love reading about idioms that have to do with different parts of the body—such as *stick out like a sore thumb* and *by a nose*.

The Idiom Connection
http://www.idiomconnection.com
The Idiom Connection has tons of easy-to-search explanations of the most common English idioms. Search alphabetically or by theme.

Idiom Site
http://www.idiomsite.com
Check out this website for an alphabetical list of expressions and what they mean.

Moses, Will. *Raining Cats & Dogs*. New York: Philomel Books, 2008. This book offers a humorous approach to investigating idioms and what they really mean.

Paint By Idioms
http://www.funbrain.com/funbrain/idioms
Play the Paint by Idioms game! Answer questions about common idioms and watch as a funny picture is painted with every correct answer.

Terban, Marvin. *In a Pickle: And Other Funny Idioms*. New York: Clarion Books, 2007. Through lively text and illustrations, Terban investigates thirty strange expressions, including *in a pickle* and *don't cry over spilled milk*.

Walton, Rick. *Why the Banana Split: An Adventure in Idioms*. Salt Lake City, Utah: Gibbs Smith, 2011. In this fictional story, Walton pokes fun at strange expressions as he tells the tale of a town threatened by a fruit-eating tyrannosaurus rex.

LERNER
e
SOURCE

Expand learning beyond the printed book. Download free, complementary educational resources for this book from our website, www.lernersource.com.

Index

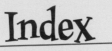

Photo Acknowledgments

The images in this book are used with the permission of: © Brand X Pictures/
Getty Images, p. 4; © Louis Fox/Digital Vision/Getty Images, p. 5; © Jonathan Ross/
Dreamstime.com, p. 6; © Yellow Dog Productions/Digital Vision/Getty Images, p. 7;
© Nick Dolding/Cultura/Getty Images, p. 8; © Verastuchelova/Dreamstime.com,
p. 9 (top); © Minden Pictures/SuperStock, p. 9 (middle); © Nigel Cattlin/Alamy, p. 9
(bottom); © Thomas Barwick/Digital Vision/Getty Images, p. 10; © iStockphoto.com/
Paul Kline, p. 11 (top); © Greg Pease/Photographer's Choice/Getty Images, p. 11
(bottom); © Vlue/Dreamstime.com, p. 12; © Royalty-Free/CORBIS, p. 13; © Ron Galella/
WireImage/Getty Images, p. 14; © Comstock Images/Getty Images, p. 15; © Skip
Nall/Photodisc/Getty Images, p. 16; © iStockphoto.com/Nancy Nehring, p. 17;
© George Doyle/Stockbyte/Getty Images, p. 19; © Wildlife/Alamy, p. 20; © Tim Hall/
Cultura/Getty Images, p. 21; © Richard Koek/Taxi/Getty Images, p. 22; The Granger
Collection, New York, p. 25 (top); © Columbia/Courtesy Everett Collection, p. 25
(bottom); © iStockphoto.com/mocker_bat, p. 26; © Universal Images Group/Getty
Images, p. 27; © The Art Gallery Collection/Alamy, p. 29.

Front cover: © ClassicStock/Alamy (orangutan); © iStockphoto.com/manley099
(graduation cap); © Todd Strand/Independent Picture Service (desk & books);
© iStockphoto.com/Steve Debenport (background).

Main body text set in Adrianna Light 11/17.
Typeface provided by Chank.